EMUS CAN'T FLY

By Chloe Daniels

Library For All Ltd.

Library For All is an Australian not for profit organisation with a mission to make knowledge accessible to all via an innovative digital library solution. Visit us at libraryforall.org

Emus Can't Fly

First published 2022

Published by Library For All Ltd
Email: info@libraryforall.org
URL: libraryforall.org

Our Yarning logo design by Jason Lee, Bidjipidji Art

Original illustrations by Caitlyn McPherson

Emus Can't Fly
Daniels, Chloe
ISBN: 978-1-922895-43-1
SKU01350

EMUS CAN'T FLY

We respect and honour Aboriginal and Torres Strait Islander Elders past, present and future. We acknowledge the stories, traditions and living cultures of Aboriginal and Torres Strait Islander peoples on this land and commit to building a brighter future together.

"Hey, crocodile, can you teach me how to fly?" asked the little emu.

"Crocodiles can't fly, but
we can swim," said the big
crocodile.

"Hey, snake, can you teach me how to fly?" asked the little emu.

"Snakes can't fly, but we can slither," said the long snake.

"Hey, koala, can you teach me how to fly?" asked the little emu.

"Koalas can't fly, but we can climb high," said the furry koala.

"Hey, kangaroo, can you teach me how to fly?" asked the little emu.

"Kangaroos can't fly, but
we can jump," said the large
kangaroo.

"Hey, lizard, can you teach me how to fly?" asked the little emu.

"Lizards can't fly, but we can scurry along," said the frilled lizard.

"Hey, dingo, can you teach me how to fly?" asked the little emu.

"Dingoes can't fly, but we can move fast," said the quick dingo.

"Hey, wombat, can you teach me how to fly?" asked the little emu.

"Wombats can't fly, but we can dig deep," said the round wombat.

Hey, echidna, can you
teach me how to fly?"
said the little emu.

"Echidnas can't fly, but we forage for ants," said the prickly echidna.

"Hey, cockatoo, can you teach me how to fly?" asked the little emu.

"Emus can't fly!" said the flapping cockatoo. "But you can run really fast!"

So the little emu ran as fast as it could, waving to the other animals as it raced by.

You can use these questions to talk about this book with your family, friends and teachers.

What did you learn from this book?

Describe this book in one word. Funny? Scary? Colourful? Interesting?

How did this book make you feel when you finished reading it?

What was your favourite part of this book?

download our reader app
getlibraryforall.org

About the author

Chloe was born in Alice Springs and lives in Darwin. She loves to hang out with family, eat food and share stories. Her favourite story is *The Very Hungry Caterpillar*.

Our Yarning

Want to discover more books from this collection? Our Yarning is a collection of books written by Aboriginal and Torres Strait Islander peoples across Australia.

We know that children learn better, and enjoy reading more, when they see themselves in the stories, characters and illustrations of the books they read.

To download the app, visit the Google Play Store on any Android device and search 'Our Yarning'.

libraryforall.org